YOU ARE AT THE HOME OF

_____

Address_____

City_____ State __

Home Phone (____)_____

Work Phone (____)_____   (____)_____
      (Mother)   (Father)

CHILDREN: Name/Nickname   Birthdate

_____ _____

_____ _____

_____ _____

IN CASE OF EMERGENCY...

Police_____ Fire Department_____

Poison Control Center_____ Ambulance_____

Nearest Hospital/Emergency Rm._____

Address_____ Phone_____

Fastest Route There_____

Doctor_____ Phone_____
          (Childrens)

Doctor_____ Phone_____
          (Family)

Drugstore/Pharmacy_____

Address_____ Phone_____

CLOSEST NEIGHBORS/RELATIVES

Name_____ Name_____

Address_____ Address_____

Phone (____)_____ Phone (____)_____

(For other important emergency phone numbers, turn the page.)

Additional Important Phone Numbers

Dentist _____
        (name)   (phone)

Electric Company _____
                (name)   (phone)

Gas Company _____
            (name)   (phone)

Furnace Company _____
                (name)   (phone)

Electrician _____
            (name)   (phone)

Taxi _____
      (name)   (phone)

Locksmith _____
          (name)   (phone)

Pet Vet _____
        (name)   (phone)

MATERNAL GRANDPARENTS   **PATERNAL GRANDPARENTS**

Name _____   Name _____

Address _____   Address _____

_____ Zip _____   _____ Zip _____

Phone (___) _____   Phone (___) _____

Other Neighbors, Friends and Relatives

_____

_____

_____

_____

_____

Dear Babysitter

HANDBOOK

Vicki Lansky

Book Peddlers
Minnetonka, MN

Editor: Kathryn Ring
Cover Design: Nancy MacLean
Production Manager: Julie Surma
Reviewers: Rebecca Kojander, P.N.P.
           Virginia Williams, P.N.P.
           Neil Meyer, J.D.

DEAR BABYSITTER HANDBOOK

PRINTING HISTORY
Meadowbrook edition/April 1982
Bantam edition/April 1987
Book Peddlers edition/October 1989

First Aid illustrations are by RMR portfolio, Minneapolis, Minnesota.
The Contents of the first-aid/medical section of this book have been
reviewed and checked for accuracy and appropriateness of application by
health-care professionals. However, the author, reviewers, and publisher
disclaim all responsibility arising from any adverse application of any of the
information. If you have any questions or concern about the appropriateness
or application of the treatments described, consult your doctor.

ISBN 0-916773-16-7

For group sales or quantity discounts contact:
Book Peddlers
15245 Minnetonka Blvd.
Minnetonka, MN 55345
612/912-0036

99 00 01 02 03 04 12 11 10 9 8

CONTENTS

Dear Parent 1

Dear Babysitter 2

What to Do When 4

A Baby Won't Stop Crying .. 4
You're Bathing a Child 4
It's Time to Eat 5
A Child Gets "Wild" 5
It's Time to Go to Bed 6

A Child Is Scared 6
A Child Won't Cooperate ... 7
There's a Temper Tantrum .. 7
Siblings Fight 8

What to Expect from Children of Different Ages 9

Birth to Six Months 10
Six to Twelve Months 12
One to Two Years 14
Two to Three Years 16

Three to Four Years 18
Four to Five Years 20
Five to Seven Years 22

Giving Medication 24

MEDICAL/FIRST AID

Medical Emergencies 26

Artificial Respiration 27
Broken Bone 28
Bumps and Bruises 29
Bumps to the Head 29
Burns 30
Choking 31
Convulsions 32
Croup 32
Cuts and Scrapes 33
Diarrhea 34

Earache 34
Fever 34
Hives 35
Nosebleeds 35
Object in Ear or Nose 35
Poisoning 36
Stings and Bites 37
Stomachache and Pain 37
Tooth Injury 38
Vomiting 38

Where to Find First-Aid Supplies 39

Allergy or Special Medical Information 40

Medical Treatment Release Form 41

Household Emergencies 43

Where to Find Household Items 45

House Rules 46

Especially for Parents 49

Easing Separation Anxiety 50

Babysitter Phone Directory 53

Dear Parent,

*B*efore you rush out for your well-deserved "time off," be sure to show your sitter this book and ask him or her to glance through it and become familiar with its contents. (It's organized so it WON'T take much time, yet WILL be helpful and informative.) You might point out the pages that you've filled out with information pertinent to your home and family.

Don't forget to write down important details for TODAY, either on a pad near the phone or at a message center (like the refrigerator). Note where you will be, a phone number if you are reachable, the time you expect to be back, and any special instructions.

If you have an infant or a child with special needs, you may have extra lengthy instructions and routines in addition to those provided in this book. If so, tuck them in this book so both you and your babysitters will become accustomed to looking in one place for everything.

To help you, your child, and the sitter deal with your leave-taking and any separation anxiety this may arouse, there are additional tips for parents on page 49.

Arrive home when you've said you will. If you're going to be late, call and let the sitter know when you will be there.

Enjoy yourself,

Vicki Lansky

1

Dear Babysitter,

*Y*ou're entrusted with the care of the most important *people in the world – MY CHILDREN. They're your priority; your job is to watch over them and keep them from danger. Please give them your undivided attention. Babysitting isn't all hard work though; you'll find that it involves lots of playing, which can be fun for you, too.*

Browse through this book so you'll know what's in it in case you need information in a hurry sometime. Pay special attention to the pages I've filled in with important details. Do your best to follow instructions about how to handle the children's wants and needs. TLC (tender, loving care!) will go a long way toward getting children to accept you as a friend.

If you're a teenager and have given up the time to take a special course in babysitting or first aid, I'm extra pleased to have you as a sitter.

If your own parents don't know exactly where you are, call them right now and give them our address and phone number. (They're on p. i of this book.)

While you are a substitute parent when I'm gone, you should abide by our "house rules," even if they're different from those of your own home. In general, please follow ordinary rules of courtesy.

- *Familiarize yourself with the house, but don't snoop in closets and drawers.*

- Don't tie up the phone; I (or others) may need to get through to you. When answering a call for me, don't say I'm not home; just tell the caller I can't answer the phone now and will call back. Please make written notes of messages and numbers for me.

- Resist refrigerator raids. If you've been told to help yourself, don't overdo it. Check the kitchen counter and the refrigerator to see if things are marked for snacks and meals.

- Leave the house as orderly as you found it – or, as the old saying goes, "Don't put things down... put them away." And wash any dishes you've used.

- Try to stay awake and alert at least until 11 or 12 p.m., unless I've told you otherwise. It's important that you be able to hear a waking child.

- Be sure to let me know of any illness or accident, however minor, and let me know if anything's been broken. Write down the details so you won't forget anything.

- If you have to break a future sitting appointment with me, please let me know as far in advance as possible (and I will do the same for you). Perhaps you might even be able to line up a substitute for me.

    Thank you!

                    Sincerely,

                    _____
                         (parent's signature)

3

WHAT TO DO WHEN ...

Plain common sense will be your best guide when you're trying to get children to do what they're supposed to do. You know that you don't like to be ordered about roughly; children don't, either. Try to be agreeable and friendly (asking for the children's help will make them feel important and may help you get them to be cooperative). Add a little humor to a situation, when you can.

Remember that you're NOT expected to be a child's parent, a doctor or a teacher. If something comes up that you just can't handle, call the parents or, in a real emergency, the appropriate outside help. (See pp. i and ii for important telephone numbers.)

When a Baby Won't Stop Crying

- First check for the obvious reasons: hunger, thirst, wetness, discomfort from being too cool or too warm, an open safety pin or a thread caught between fingers or toes.

- Then try one or more of the classic calmers: warmth; different, soothing sounds; or motion. Wrap the baby in a receiving blanket and hold him or her close to your body; turn up music on the radio or stereo; walk or dance with the baby; put the baby in a wind-up swing. If nothing works put the baby in the crib for a few minutes and give yourself a breather. Then try again.

When You're Bathing a Child

- If you're bathing a baby, follow the parents' instructions carefully. Have a big towel handy (perhaps clipped around your neck) to receive the wet, slippery little body.

4

- NEVER leave a child you're bathing in the tub alone. Let the phone or doorbell ring, or wrap the child in a towel and take him or her with you.

- Try to make a game of bathing if a child is afraid of the bath. Run the water before taking the child into the bathroom and use only a few inches of water in the tub.

- Check occasionally an older child who's bathing alone just to be sure everything's all right.

When It's Time to Eat

- If you're feeding an infant, see p. 10 for tips on bottles and burping.

- Allow plenty of time for small children; they're often slow eaters. Expect a certain amount of messiness and don't worry about manners, unless an older child is out of control.

- If a child won't eat, don't worry. Offer food (but not dessert) a little later, and don't make a big deal of it.

- Be sure to watch a child in a high chair carefully. Fasten belts or straps securely; don't turn your back on the child; and don't let him or her stand up in the high chair.

When a Child Gets "Wild"

- First of all, try to head off too much excitement for a child; mix quiet activities with strenuous ones.

WHAT TO DO WHEN . . .

- When you can't avoid excitement, slow the pace with active but not wild play—a run around the outside of the house or a game of strength.

- Offer a snack, sitting down at the table, to help calm a child.

When It's Time to Go to Bed

- Avoid rough play and running games before bedtime; excitement makes it hard for children to sleep. Promise a story, once the child is under the covers.

- Check a sleeping child once an hour or so, and check an infant more frequently. Keep TV, radio or stereo turned down so you can hear a child who wakes.

- NEVER leave children—even soundly sleeping ones—alone in the house.

When a Child Is Scared

- Don't laugh at a child who's scared of anything—the dark, thunder, "monsters." Treat the child's fear seriously and do what you can to reassure him or her.

- Try leaving a night-light on for a child afraid of the dark; "boom back" at thunder; blow monsters out the window or flush them down the toilet.

- Tell the child about some of the fears you had when you were little and how you were able to overcome them.

When a Child Won't Cooperate

- Try to avoid putting a child in a position where he or she can say "NO." Give face-saving commands like "How about ... ?" or "Shall we ... ?" instead of "Now you must ..." And give choices when you can: "Do you want to do this now, or after your nap?"

- It's best not to use physical punishment on a child you're sitting for unless the parents have told you a light slap on the hand or a spank to the behind is all right in some circumstances. Instead, look sternly and directly into the child's eyes, send a misbehaving child to his or her room, forbid TV or another pleasure or threaten to tell the parents when they return (but then you'd better DO IT; children catch on to idle threats very quickly).

Don't jerk a child by the arm or pull him or her up by the arm only—you could easily dislocate an elbow.

When There's a Temper Tantrum

- Ignore a tantrum if you can; when there's no audience, it's not much fun. If you have to notice it, try to distract the child by doing or saying something silly or by whispering to him or her so screaming will have to stop if you're to be heard.

- Or put the child in his or her crib or room, or leave the room (briefly) yourself.

- If the child is still angry when the tantrum stops, help him or her work it out by doing something physical, such as hitting a tree with a stick, punching a pillow or doing vigorous exercises.

When Siblings Fight

- Brothers and sisters often squabble just to get attention. Ignore fighting if you can, unless a bigger child is hurting a smaller one. In that case, you'll have to intervene.

- Separate the children by putting them in different rooms or on opposite sides of the same room, and get each one interested in a different activity.

- Or suggest an activity that you can all do together to take their minds off the fight.

- Don't make judgments about who is right or wrong; if you take sides, you will only make one child or the other angry.

WHAT TO EXPECT FROM CHILDREN OF DIFFERENT AGES

On the following pages, you'll find descriptions of the general characteristics you may expect to see in children of various ages. Don't be surprised, though, if the children you babysit for don't always "match" the descriptions exactly. No two children develop at the same rate, either physically or mentally. Each child is unique, just as each teenager and adult is.

Some ideas for things to do for fun with children of different ages are also included. You'll find that there will be overlap in the things children like to do; sometimes preschoolers like to play "baby games" and a two-year-old may like to attempt something (briefly!) he or she is not able to do well yet.

Many sitters like to make up their own entertainment or "surprise" bags or boxes to provide something new and different for the children they sit with. Your assortment need not be expensive and you can add and subtract things as you get new ideas. Some possibilities are pipe cleaners, whistles, balloons, magnets, cardboard cores from paper towels and toilet tissue, fabric scraps, bits of yarn, puzzles you make yourself by pasting bright pictures on cardboard and cutting into simple shapes—you'll think of lots of things as you get to know the children you babysit for.

From Birth to Six Months Old

Infants need lots of loving care; they're just made to be cuddled and rocked (a rocking chair is a wonderful piece of furniture!), and they can't be spoiled by too much attention. Each baby's style is unique; it's not your "fault" if one cries, is wakeful or won't take a bottle.

A baby up to about three months may suffer from colic – severe cramping of the digestive tract. The baby pulls his or her legs up, clenches fists, may flush bright red, and cries very hard. Try using some of the ideas on p. 4 to soothe a crying baby.

When you check infants to see if they're comfortable, you'll find their hands cool; feel their arms, legs or neck instead. Don't wear jewelry or dangly earrings that could cut or bruise tender skin or that a baby can grab. And when you lift or hold a tiny one, remember to support the wobbly little head with one hand.

Don't ever turn your back on a baby on a changing table. Even tiny ones "scoot about" if they're crying hard, and if you're caring for an older one, the very moment  you're not looking may be the time he or she learns to roll over. If you're nervous about changing or dressing a baby, do it on a soft blanket on the floor.

Don't prop a bottle on a pillow or anything else for an infant; milk won't flow evenly if the bottle slips and there's always a possibility the baby may choke. Remember to burp the infant once or twice during a feeding and after it. The simplest way to burp a baby is to hold him or her on your shoulder with a diaper underneath and gently pat the back between the shoulder blades.

Between three and six months, babies begin to smile, coo, babble and look at everything with great interest. As they begin to be able to clasp and gum things, watch for what they can reach and put into their mouths.

Things to Do for Fun

- The best entertainment for a baby this age is simply to be held and rocked and cuddled.

- Make interesting sounds for the baby to listen to: the crumpling of stiff paper, the tinkle of a spoon on a cup, the humming of your own voice.

- With the baby on your knees, holding his or her hands firmly, play "ride-a-cock-horse," bouncing gently.

- Babies like to look at bright colors (red and yellow are favorites) and faces (eyes are fascinating to them).

- Even infants like a change of scenery; at about three months they love to be propped in infant seats (with safety belt secured!). For extra safety, set the infant seat on the floor.

- Spend lots of time reading, singing and talking to young babies, and don't worry about their level of understanding.

- Newborns will grasp anything you put in their palms; older babies like to shake rattles and pull on or bat at objects you hold for them.

- Be sure to get down to a baby's level often, so you don't always look like a giant!

Six to Twelve Months Old

ACTIVE is the word for six- to twelve-month-old babies. During this period, most begin to push themselves backward and forward, kick vigorously, creep, crawl and pull themselves up on furniture. Many try to cruise about the house with one hand gripping or resting on anything available and, by about a year, some can stagger about without support. They learn to climb, too – stairs become fascinating.

You'll discover that these babies are so busy that they may be hard to dress and clean up. You need to watch them every waking hour and be alert for anything they can reach or grab.

Children at this age can hold their own bottles and they learn to drink from cups. They can stuff food into their mouths with some accuracy and may want to "assist" you in feeding by holding their own spoons.

Six- to twelve-month-old babies are learning words. They know their own names and those of family members and pets; they're also familiar with words for common objects in their worlds – "shoe," "ball," "juice." And they're beginning to say words – "da-da" and "bye-bye" often come first.

Generally, they're sociable little creatures, but at some point around eight months, they may begin to show what the experts call "stranger anxiety." A child who welcomed you with joy last week may shy away from you and show fear when you arrive this week. Don't take it personally. Like so many other things, "it's just a stage."

Teething usually begins during this time, though some babies get teeth even earlier. A teething baby is often cross and cranky and will gnaw on anything from a nice suitable teething biscuit or plastic ring to a crib rail or shoe sole – even on YOU!

Things to Do for Fun

- Read, sing and talk to babies this age, and be alert for their attempts to reply or join you.

- Let them look at themselves in a mirror, but YOU hold it if it's glass.

- Any of the old nursery games you remember will be amusing – "pat-a-cake," "peek-a-boo," "this little piggy."

- For more active play, these babies love repetition: they will drop things from the crib, playpen or walker for you to pick up (endlessly!). They also enjoy reaching for objects and grabbing things from your hand.

- Roll a ball back and forth between you and the baby, and teach the baby to pull something forward on a blanket. Or hide a toy under the blanket and let the baby find it.

- Another good activity is to give the child a number of small objects to put into and take out of a box or basket.

- If it's allowed by the parents, the baby loves to play with pots, pans and plastic containers in the kitchen.

One to Two Years Old

Children from one to two years old are extremely active and mobile and are usually able to run with confidence by the end of this period. They're curious about everything and they want to try every new activity they can think of, from pulling the tablecloth off the table to climbing a full flight of stairs (without knowing how to get back down). They like to look out windows, especially if there's activity going on outdoors. It's up to you to be sure they can't fall out.

"Getting into things" is perfectly normal at this age; you must set the limits of what you know is permitted and safe. Everything that can fit into a little mouth may end up there, even nasty-smelling or -tasting medicines and household cleaners, so beware! You'll see a lot of dropping, banging and throwing. But there will also be wet, sticky kisses and big bear hugs for a patient, loving sitter.

As they near two, children often show signs of being totally negative, saying "NO" to everything and doing the opposite of what they're asked to do. Your "don't touch" or "come here" will have little effect; you'll do better by  distracting a child with a toy, luring him or her to you in some way, or simply picking up and moving the child. If you're faced with a full-scale temper tantrum, don't panic; try some of the ideas on p. 7.

Children this age can be delightful, too. They understand a great many words and are usually speaking in sentences by age two. They're beginning to show independence and want to do whatever they can on their own.

Things to Do for Fun

- One- to two-year-olds love to have an audience as they play "make believe" with toy telephones, miniature cars, trucks and dolls.

- Simple puzzles, stacking toys and objects to take apart and put together are big favorites.

- Try building a tower of blocks; the child will enjoy knocking it down again and again.

- Ball rolling and retrieving is also fun; it's safest to use a ball made of spongy material so no one will get hurt if it's thrown.

- At quiet time and before bedtime you'll read a lot to this child, and he or she will probably request the same books again and again.

- You may find that a child this age has a security blanket or a favorite toy which goes everywhere the child goes – especially into bed.

- Make pick-up time a game by letting the child toss whichever toys he or she chooses into a basket, holding it a little farther away each time.

- Play simple "hide-and-seek" by stooping behind a chair where the child can see part of your body. Let him or her "find" you. You can hide a doll or stuffed animal, too.

- If you can find a big cardboard box, turn it on its side and let the child crawl in and out and hide from you.

Two to Three Years Old

Children from two to three are seldom still. They're inquisitive and like to experiment with things that come apart or are breakable, so they need to be closely watched.

"NO" may still be a favorite word for two-year-olds; these children can be domineering, demanding, stubborn and rigid. They resent your "DON'TS"; they want WHAT they want, WHEN they want it. Try some of the ideas on p. 7 if a child won't do what he or she is supposed to do. Sometimes it may be necessary to ignore the child's fussing and go on as if there were no problems, perhaps

offering a little reward when the activity is finished.

Toilet training is usually underway about this time. Just do your best, following whatever method the parents have established, and don't make a big deal of accidents.

As they get closer to three, children usually become more cooperative and show more self-control. You'll hear "yes," and "we," offered in a spirit of cooperation. A child will be able to carry on a real conversation with you and will ask hundreds of questions, sometimes just to "test" you, but often to get real information.

Imagination develops rapidly. Role playing begins at about this age, and many children have imaginary playmates that you may have to include at meals and tuck into bed.

Things to Do for Fun

- Children this age like to work puzzles and play with construction toys.

- They enjoy scribbling on paper (and walls – beware!) with crayons and markers; they also like to string beads, shape playdough and make paper chains.

- They're able to handle pegboards and other sorting and matching toys.

- They'll be fascinated by puppet shows you might invent for them to take part in.

- And making "music" with rhythm instruments is lots of fun for them; if real instruments aren't available, banging on a tin can with a wooden spoon is just as good.

- Outdoors, the sandbox holds endless possibilities, and children love water play with plastic cups for pouring and measuring. Or try taking a walk if the weather is fine.

- For quiet time, try to remember finger games you used to play, like "itsy-bitsy spider," and counting songs, like "this old man." Children's television programs may be of interest to a child this age, but probably only for short periods. During reading time, the child will begin to point to things in pictures and talk with you about the story.

Three to Four Years Old

Children this age are learning to do a wide variety of things very well – ride tricycles; throw, kick and catch balls; climb and play on jungle gyms and seesaws; hop and balance on one foot. They still need to be watched carefully outdoors; they may "forget" about the dangers of the street or wander away from home. By 4, they're more independent and may be allowed to play outdoors alone (ask the parents for permission), but they still need to be checked on fairly often.

Many experts believe that pretending reaches a peak during this year. Children talk to themselves, their toys, pets, imaginary friends – and YOU. Vivid imaginations often lead to a variety of fears – try some of the ideas on p. 6 when you have a scared child on your hands. Children often have nightmares at this age, and the best response is to wake the child from the bad dream and comfort him or her as best you can.

Children this age are also learning to play with other children. A year ago, these children would play alone while in the same room or grab things from each other while playing together. Now they interact more and enjoy each other's company. They may quarrel sometimes, too, about whose turn it is and who may play with what toy.

Things to Do for Fun

- The three- to four-year-old will enjoy role playing with you; he or she likes to play "house," "store," "school."

- Clay, crayons and paper, coloring books, finger paints, chalk and chalkboards, blunt scissors, and paste are all popular materials – but watch the scissors; they can cut hair and clothes as well as paper.

- You can help or watch a child of this age work a puzzle, and you can play simple two-person games like "Lotto" and "Candyland" with the child. Other traditional favorites are "Simon says" and "statues."

- The child's attention span may be short during either reading or television watching, but he or she will often return to these activities after a few minutes of play with something else.

- In good weather, try taking a walk outdoors to collect leaves, stones or pine cones; see how many nature items the child can identify. City children enjoy watching for buses and fire engines and looking for other children.

- Have the child lie down on a big piece of wrapping paper and draw an outline of his or her whole body. Watch or help as the child draws in the face, hair and clothes.

- Help the child make a fort out of a blanket or bedspread stretched over two or three chairs indoors or hung over a clothesline outdoors. Or make a bus out of a line of chairs and stools and let the child be the driver who takes you and a few stuffed animals and dolls to far-away places.

- Play simple dice games (as simple as rolling two dice to see who gets the highest total) with children this age; dice are easier for them to handle than cards.

Four to Five Years Old

Four- to five-year-olds are quite independent; they don't like to be treated as "babies." Often they insist on doing things their own way. They develop new and strong likes and dislikes for food, playmates, clothes and toys, and they switch these preferences often and unpredictably.

They can wash and dress themselves, brush their own teeth and go to the bathroom alone most of the time. They may cooperate with you in picking up their toys, but don't plan on it – you probably don't have quite the authority the parents have. Children this age like to show you where things are in their homes, help you prepare simple meals and tell you "how things are done." Don't accept all this blindly – they're smart enough to try to fool you sometimes!

These children can hop, skip and turn somersaults and cartwheels. They're also able to hit, kick, scream and throw things. "Bathroom humor," the use of "dirty" words and inappropriate behavior, often appears about this time. It's usually best to ignore it; a big show of either shock or amusement only makes it more fun for the child.

Imagination is still developing in these children; role playing also continues to interest them. Sometimes the line between fact and fiction is thin, and you may be told many "stories."

Things to Do for Fun

- All the indoor activities and craft work that three-year-olds like are still popular with these children, but they can do them better now and will spend more time with them. You should still expect some messiness.

- In addition, they're showing interest in letters and numbers and like to play word and math games. Some can even entertain you by "reading" (often from memory) their books to you. If they go to nursery school or Sunday school, they may be learning new skills to show you.

- Try an enjoyable quiet game to stimulate imagination: ask a child, "If you could have one wish, what would it be?" and then speculate with the child about what would happen if the wish came true.

- Active play outdoors – hopscotch, hide and seek, tricycle riding and timed runs around the house – are good ways for a child to work off steam. Expect lots of noise and activity, especially if other children are present.

- Make hats and masks for dress-up play from large paper bags. Cut holes for eyes and mouth and help the child color the masks to represent story-book characters or scary creatures.

- Do simple calisthenics (just bending, stretching and reaching are fine) or dance with the child when you must be indoors and feel that some exercise would be a good change of pace.

- Look through the family album with the child and let him or her point out pictures of friends and family members and tell you about them.

Five to Seven Years Old

You may be astonished at how reliable, stable and well-adjusted some five-year-olds are. These children can take care of their own physical needs, pick up and put away their clothes and possessions and behave according to their parents' rules. They're apt to be proud of their appearance, their families and their homes. You may be needed only occasionally for help, advice or friendship.

At about the age of 5½ or 6, though, the same children may become as indecisive and demanding as 2½-year-olds. They may dawdle at meals and tasks and act rude, resistant and moody. You may hear things like, "I don't have to mind you, you're not my mother." Some helpful phrases to use at these times are: "See if you can do it before I count to 10," "Just try it this way," "A good thing to do is .... " A child this age may know how to tell time, or at least is probably learning; try using a kitchen timer to reinforce the sense of time and get a slowpoke moving.

Seven-year-olds often begin to be more independent. They like to be alone sometimes, reading, watching television or listening to records. Sometimes they're perfectionists; they'll do something over and over until they're pleased with it. When they're absorbed in an activity they won't "hear" you and they "forget" lots of things.

Children this age often seem to enjoy complaining and feeling bad. They're picked on ... "it's not fair" ... nobody likes them ... they're going to run away from home. Your best bet is to be sympathetic but to let them be alone if that's what they want, or to suggest something interesting to do together, if they prefer company.

Things to Do for Fun

- You may actually spend less time entertaining children of this age than you do younger ones, since they often play by themselves or with friends. You'll need to learn the parents' rules about where the children may go and whether they may have visitors.

- Outdoors they're active – they jump rope, play running games and ride bikes. They may like to have you join them, or they may be happiest alone or with friends.

- These children like to read to you and with you – comics and newspaper comics are popular – and they usually love riddles, so try to remember all the good ones you can.

- Dressing dolls and playing dress-up keep girls busy for hours; boys often like to manipulate tools and play with construction toys. But don't think ANY activity is limited to either sex!

- Look at a big catalog with the child and let him or her pick out things that would be fun to have. "Spend" certain amounts, in total, such as $10, $25 or $100.

- They'll enjoy playing board games with you, and they want to WIN, so be prepared for some cheating. If you want to let a child win without cheating, create a handicap system. For example, make a rule that in checkers you change sides of the board every two or three moves.

- Make up a silly story with the child. You start a sentence, let him or her finish it.

Giving Medication

When you give medication to a child, be very careful to follow any instructions you've been given. The parents may also give you ideas of the best ways to get ALL of a dose of medicine into a child. Here are some good ways.

- Give a baby medicine in a nipple; he or she will suck it out. Don't put it in a bottle of milk or formula; you won't know how much of the medicine has been taken if the baby doesn't finish the bottle.
- Measure carefully! Use a regular medicine spoon if the parents have one, or a teaspoon or tablespoon from a set of measuring spoons. Spoons from the tableware aren't accurate.
- Try buttering a pill to make it slip down easily, or bury it in a spoonful of applesauce or jam. Or put it in a spoon and crush it with another, then mix it with the applesauce or jam.
- Follow the medicine with a glass of the child's favorite liquid, if you're sure it's all right to do so.

Be sure to put medicine container caps back on securely and to put containers back in a safe place, out of reach of children.

If you're caring for an infant or small child, the parents may have liquid Tylenol on hand. If you're giving Tylenol, follow instructions on the container, unless the parents have given you specific instructions.

If you are giving children's chewable, 80-milligram aspirin, the following dosages are recommended (every four hours):

- Infants, as directed by doctor (or parents).
- Ages 1 to 2, one tablet.
- Ages 2 and 3, two tablets.
- Ages 4 and 5, three tablets.
- Ages 6 to 8, four tablets.

MEDICAL/FIRST AID ✚

Artificial Respiration 27
Broken Bone 28
Bumps and Bruises 29
Bumps to the Head 29
Burns 30
Choking 31
Convulsions 32
Croup 32
Cuts and Scrapes 33
Diarrhea 34
Earache 34
Fever 34
Hives 35
Nosebleeds 35
Object in Ear or Nose 35
Poisoning 36
Stings and Bites 37
Stomachache and Pain 37
Tooth Injury 38
Vomiting 38

Medical Emergencies

> *If a child is UNCONSCIOUS, has TROUBLE BREATHING, has lost a great deal of BLOOD or has VERY SEVERE BURNS, call the AMBULANCE immediately. (The phone number is on p. i of this book.)*

While you probably won't ever actually have to save a child's life, it's best to be prepared for both minor and major emergencies. The first-aid section of this book lists many of the illnesses and injuries most common in children and also tells you when you should call a DOCTOR, a DENTIST, the POISON CONTROL CENTER or the PARENTS of the child you're sitting for. Look through pp. 24 through 38 so you'll know what's here, in case you need it. Familiarize yourself with the first-aid supplies in the house (see p. 39); find out where they are and what they are used for so that in a moment of panic you won't give a child the wrong treatment or medicine.

Remember that the best thing you can do for an ill or injured child is to remain calm yourself. Offer sympathy and consideration – and remember that simple TLC will make a child feel better almost every time.

If you call a doctor or dentist and get an answering service (likely on weekends and at night), be sure to explain that this is an emergency; tell who you are, where you are, what has happened and what number you can be reached at. Whoever you call, try to speak slowly and clearly, explain things as simply as you can, and don't hang up until the other party has a chance to ask you any necessary questions. Listen very carefully to any instructions you're given and do exactly what you're told to do.

If a child must be taken to the hospital emergency room, you may have to call a cab to get there, or ask a neighbor or your own parents for help. You may need to provide a medical treatment release form to authorize treatment. Take this book along; a form, signed and ready for use, is on p. 41.

✚ Artificial Respiration

If a baby or child is not breathing, CALL THE AMBU-LANCE IMMEDIATELY. Begin artificial respiration (mouth-to-mouth resuscitation) by laying the child on the floor or another firm surface. Put one hand on the chin tilting head to neutral or slightly backward position.

For a Baby or Very Small Child

• Place your mouth over the child's mouth and nose, making an airtight seal.

For an Older Child

• Cover the child's mouth with your mouth, making an airtight seal.
• Pinch the child's nose closed, or be sure your cheek closes the nose.

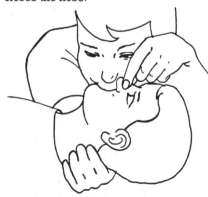

Then

• Give slow, gentle breaths into the child's mouth, one every three seconds.
• Pause after first breath to take in a replenishing oxygen-rich breath.
• Look to see the chest rise as breath is grown. If chest does not rise, child's airway may be blocked.
  • If chest does not rise and fall, repeat until the child starts to breath normally or until help arrives.

✚ Broken Bone

If a child falls and hurts an arm, leg or collarbone and seems to be in great pain, you can suspect that a bone has been broken. Even if you aren't sure there's been a break, it's safest to treat the child as if there has been.

- Keep the child still and warm, and don't move him or her unless it's absolutely necessary.
- If you must move the child, try to support the broken-bone area with a homemade splint. Slip a big, soft pillow or folded blanket under the limb. Wrap it over the limb, then bind it in place with a belt, elastic bandage, piece of cloth or string.

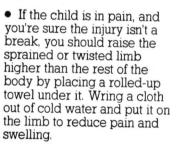

- If the child is in pain, and you're sure the injury isn't a break, you should raise the sprained or twisted limb higher than the rest of the body by placing a rolled-up towel under it. Wring a cloth out of cold water and put it on the limb to reduce pain and swelling.

- CALL THE PARENTS.

- Keep the injured limb in as natural a position as possible, without moving it, while you and the child wait for help. Offer aspirin or Tylenol if you have the approval of the parents to do so. (See p. 24 for dosage, if the parents haven't told you how much to give.)

✚ Bumps and Bruises

More frightening than serious (to both you and a child) are the many minor accidents children have. However, you should write down all the details of the accident so the parents can watch for further symptoms. In most cases, a show of concern on your part will make the child feel better immediately. Don't act angry at the fact that a child "shouldn't have done that" or "should have been more careful."

- Apply a cold compress to ease the pain and reduce swelling. One good one is a clean towel or washcloth wrung out of cold water.

- Or try an ice cube wrapped in a washcloth or a can of frozen juice covered with a dry cloth so the child can hold it on the hurting spot.

✚ Bumps to the Head

Bumps to the head look worse than others because there is no place for the swelling to go but outward, where it shows. The cold compress described above will relieve the pain and swelling of most head bumps, but a serious blow to the head may mean that the child has had a concussion.

CALL THE DOCTOR if you see any of these signs of serious head injury (they may take as long as two hours to appear, so watch the child carefully):

- **Unconsciousness, being "knocked out" or inability to remember what happened.**

- PERSISTENT vomiting (vomiting once or twice is fairly common after a bump to the head).

- Loss of the use of an arm or leg.

- Increasing irritability.

- Blurred vision, inability to see for any length of time after the bump, or unequal pupil size in the two eyes.

- Bleeding from either ear.

- Increasing sleepiness; you're unable to rouse the child.

✚ Burns

There are different kinds of burns: MINOR, in which the skin is unbroken and not blistered; MORE SEVERE, in which skin is blistered; and VERY SEVERE, in which much of the body is burned badly.

Never pull off clothing which is stuck to a burned area. Cover the area with a cold, wet cloth.

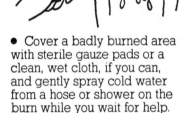

- If the burn is minor or if there is only a small, unbroken blister, run cold water over it for about five minutes, or until the pain stops. Or cover the burn with a towel or washcloth wrung out of cold water or hold an ice cube wrapped in a cloth on it.

- Cover a badly burned area with sterile gauze pads or a clean, wet cloth, if you can, and gently spray cold water from a hose or shower on the burn while you wait for help.

A burn caused by a child biting an electric cord is an emergency. Call the doctor immediately.

- If a burn is severe, with broken or heavily blistered skin (especially on hands or face), or if it covers an area of the child's body larger than his or her hand, CALL THE DOCTOR. DO NOT break a blister.

- Give the child as much water as he or she will drink – it will provide a distraction and will also help to prevent dehydration, a danger with a bad burn. Offer aspirin or Tylenol, if you've been authorized to do so. (See **p. 24** for dosages if you haven't been given them.)

✚ Choking

If a child has swallowed something and is coughing hard, let the coughing continue. This is the body's way of getting rid of a foreign object in the throat or windpipe. If the child can't talk, breathe or cough at all, do the following things:

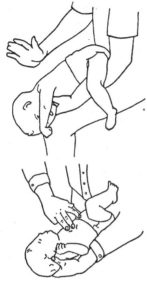

For a Baby or Very Small Child

• Hold the child upside down in a jackknife position.

• Give several quick blows to the child's back, between the shoulder blades with the heel of your hand.

• Repeat as necessary, until the swallowed object "pops out."

OR

• Position an infant face up on your forearm.

• Use two or three fingers positioned centrally below the nipples and give five quick thrusts by pushing down about one inch.

• Repeat if necessary.

For an Older Child

• Use the "Heimlich hug." Stand behind the child and wrap your arms around his or her waist.

• Make a fist with one of your hands and grab it with the other hand.

• Place the fist against the child's abdomen, slightly above the navel and below the rib cage. PRESS into the abdomen with a QUICK, UPWARD THRUST.

• Repeat at short intervals, if necessary, until the object is ejected.

If none of these methods work, CALL 911 and continue to work on the child until help comes.

31

✚ Convulsions

If a child's body stiffens up and starts jerking, perhaps with eyes rolled back into the head, the child may be having a convulsion. It can be frightening, but don't panic – it's usually over very quickly.

- Watch the child carefully and note which parts of the body are jerking – the doctor will want to know everything possible about the seizure.

- Lay the child down where he or she can't get hurt.

- DO NOT put a spoon in the child's mouth, even if you've heard that's the right thing to do.

- Turn the child's head to the side if he or she is drooling, to prevent choking.

- CALL THE DOCTOR.

When the convulsion is over, loosen the child's clothing, especially around the neck.

If the child stops breathing, start artificial respiration. (See p. 27 for instructions.)

✚ Croup

Croup usually appears at night. The child who has it coughs very hard with a "barking" sound that can be frightening, wheezes, and may have a hard time breathing and swallowing.. The child may drool and there may be a bluish tinge around his or her mouth.

- Offer water, if you're sure the child will be able to swallow it.

- Get the child into warm, moist air as soon as possible. The best and quickest way is to hold him or her on your lap in the bathroom, with the door closed and very hot water running in the tub or shower, for 10 or 15 minutes.

- If the wheezing and difficult breathing continue, and if the weather outdoors is cool and moist, dress the child warmly and carry him or her out, where the natural cool humidity can relieve the symptoms.

- CALL THE PARENTS. Or, if the symptoms are very severe and breathing continues to be difficult, CALL THE DOCTOR FIRST.

✚ Cuts and Scrapes

A cut or scrape can be very upsetting to a child, especially if it bleeds a lot. The two important things to remember are:

> **Stop bleeding by applying pressure. Clean the wound, if possible.**

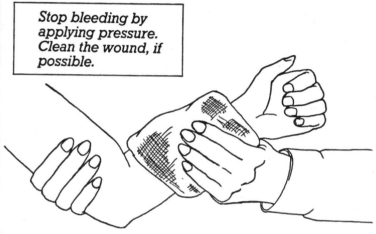

• To stop bleeding, apply pressure directly on the wound with a clean cloth (a dark one will "hide" the blood). Press firmly and continuously for about five minutes or until bleeding stops. Add more cloth on top if necessary. If you can, raise the injured part higher than the child's head; this makes bleeding stop more quickly.

• NEVER try to use a tourniquet unless you've been properly trained to. You could do more harm than good.

• Once bleeding stops, clean a cut gently with soap and water. DO NOT try to dig out glass or other sharp materials.

• Apply an antiseptic such as Bactine, but put it on the bandage, not the wound, so it won't sting or hurt the child.

> **If a cut looks very deep or wide after bleeding stops, or if bleeding doesn't stop, CALL THE PARENTS. Stitches or other medical attention may be necessary.**

✚ Diarrhea

Diarrhea is usually nothing more than a mess and a nuisance; in most cases you don't have to worry about it. Do not offer the child milk or juice to drink. And do be sure to tell the parents about it when they return; they'll want to watch for other symptoms. If it's very severe and attacks continue for several hours, CALL THE PARENTS.

✚ Earache

If a child complains of pain in the ear, keep him or her in a sitting position, not lying down. If the parents have authorized you to give the child medicine when you're in charge, offer aspirin or Tylenol (see p. 24 for dosages) and put a few drops of warm earache oil in the ear. The best way to warm the oil is to stand the container in hot water for a few minutes.

✚ Fever

A child with a high fever has glassy eyes; a flushed, hot body; rapid, shallow breathing; and an increased heartbeat.

- DO NOT try to take a rectal temperature unless you have been trained to do so – an inexperienced person can injure a baby or small child.

- Offer lots of liquid and, if you've been told you may, aspirin or Tylenol (dosages are on p. 24).

- Apply a cool, damp cloth to the child's forehead or put the child into a tub of lukewarm water, pour water over his or her body and rub the body briskly with a washcloth.

- A child whose fever rises very rapidly may go into a convulsion (see p. 32).

- If you think the fever may be very high, CALL THE PARENTS.

✚ Hives

If a child breaks out in hives (they look like red bumps with white centers) or begins to itch a great deal, he or she may be having an allergic reaction. Check p. 40 to see if the parents have given special instructions for an allergy. The parents may have a lotion available to stop itching (see p. 39), or you might try putting the child in a tub of lukewarm water with a handful of baking soda added. Be sure to tell the parents about it when they return.

✚ Nosebleeds

Nosebleeds may be caused by colds, allergies or dried-out membranes in the nose. They're frightening to children because of the blood, but rarely serious. You'll want to stop one as quickly as you can. Do not let the child lie down; he or she may swallow the blood and choke. Have him or her sit down, then:

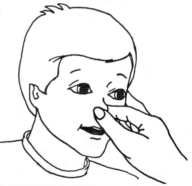

• Lean the trunk of the child's body forward.

• Squeeze the child's nostrils together firmly and continuously for about five minutes, or until bleeding has stopped.

• Keep the child quiet to prevent renewed bleeding.

• If bleeding continues and can't be stopped, CALL THE PARENTS.

✚ Object in Ear or Nose

Small children seem to be especially fond of putting things in their noses and ears. Don't try to prod or pry anything out unless you can see it easily; you may only push it farther in. CALL THE PARENTS and get their instructions.

✚ Poisoning

While many medicines, cleaning agents, houseplants and cosmetics are not poisonous, it's best to assume they are if a child gets into them. If you suspect a child of having swallowed something poisonous, act quickly, before the poison can take effect.

• Find out exactly what the child swallowed, if you don't know. Try to locate the container the substance came from or a leaf of a plant that's been eaten. If the child vomits, try to save a sample of the vomit. Check for such signs as unusual smells, burns in the mouth, stains on the child's **clothes, or strange behavior** (confusion, sleepiness, anxiety, stomach pain).

• Then CALL THE POISON CONTROL CENTER. (See the inside front page for number.) Speak slowly and clearly and mention all the things you've noticed. Don't hang up until you've been given instructions and been asked any necessary questions.

• Follow instructions very carefully. You may be told to give the child water or milk to drink, to dilute the poison, or to try to make the child vomit, using syrup of ipecac (see p. 39) or another method. DON'T FORCE VOMITING UNLESS YOU'RE SPECIFICALLY TOLD TO; it may be harmful in some cases.

When you've done everything you can, call the parents.

• If a poisonous substance has gotten into a child's eye or on his or her skin, wash the area with lukewarm water. Hold the child's face under a faucet, if necessary, but protect nose and mouth so water won't run in.

• If the child has inhaled poisonous fumes, open the windows or take the child out into fresh air immediately.

✚ Stings and Bites

Insect stings and bites are itchy and sometimes even painful. The parents may have on hand a soothing lotion or ointment (see p. 39), or you can make a paste of baking soda and water. Use a small amount of baking soda and just enough water to make a thick paste that will stay on the skin.

- For bee, wasp or hornet stings, use a baking-soda paste or hold ice, wrapped in a cloth, on the sting to reduce swelling. If the stinger is still in the child's skin, try to pull it out with tweezers after the swelling goes down.

- If a child shows an allergic reaction to a bee sting (large swelling, puffy eyes, difficulty in breathing), GO TO THE EMERGENCY ROOM IMMEDIATELY.

- For animal or "people" bites, wash the bitten area with soap and cool running water so all the saliva is rinsed off. If the skin is broken, apply an antiseptic such as Bactine. Cover the bite with a clean cloth, keep the child quiet and CALL THE PARENTS.

- If you've seen the animal, or if you know who it belongs to, be sure to tell the parents immediately. Prompt action must be taken to isolate the animal, especally if it's a dog or cat, in case it has rabies. (Squirrels, chipmunks, gerbils and guinea pigs do not carry rabies.)

✚ Stomachache and Pain

It's very common for children to have stomachaches; they often mean nothing more than that the child has to go to the bathroom. Sometimes they're reactions to even minor stress such as having been left behind by the parents.

- Touch or rub the child's abdomen gently and find out just where the pain is located. (The first common symptoms of appendicitis, for which you'd CALL THE DOCTOR, are fever, nausea and vomiting, with pain at first all over the abdomen, then on just the right side.) If the abdomen is tender to the touch or feels hard or swollen, have the child lie down and don't offer food or water

- CALL THE PARENTS if pain seems very severe or lasts for more than an hour or two. And tell them about even mild pain when they return so they can watch for further symptoms. **37**

✚ Tooth Injury

It's not uncommon for a child to knock out a tooth in a fall or bump, especially a baby tooth.

- If the whole tooth, root and all, is knocked out, the dentist may be able to put it back in place, but SPEED IS IMPORTANT. CALL THE DENTIST (see p. ii) or get the child to the EMERGENCY ROOM.

- Save the tooth by wrapping it carefully in a damp cloth or tissue or putting it into a jar of water. Don't wipe it off or try to clean it.

- If the child is in pain, offer water and, if you've been told you may, aspirin or Tylenol (dosages are on p. 24).

✚ Vomiting

It's upsetting when a child throws up, but don't show disgust or anger about it – the child doesn't like it any better than you do. Simply comfort him or her as best you can and quickly clean up the mess. (A solution of a cup of water with a tablespoon of baking soda added will help remove the odor.) Try to help the child get to the bathroom if there's repeated vomiting, or have him or her lie down with a large bowl or towel handy for "accidents."

- Don't offer food or even water for at least an hour after vomiting stops; either may start it up again. Instead, have the child rinse out his or her mouth with water and spit it out. When vomiting has stopped, sucking a few ice chips will help relieve the dryness of the child's mouth.

- Sometimes infants vomit even when they aren't sick. A little "spitting up" is very common. You may see what's called "projectile vomiting" after a feeding – an immediate cascade of milk, thrown up in an arc. If it happens only once, don't worry (but do let the parents know about it when they return). If it happens after two or more feedings, or if the baby vomits violently, instead of just spitting up, CALL THE PARENTS.

WHERE
TO FIND
First-Aid Supplies

Syrup Of Ipecac _____
<small>(for poisoning; DO NOT give ipecac unless you are told to)</small>

Activated Charcoal _____
<small>(also for poisoning; DO NOT use unless you are told to)</small>

Band-Aids, Bandages, Antiseptic _____

Children's Aspirin, Tylenol _____
<small>**(follow dosages p. 24)**</small>

Thermometer _____
<small>(don't take a rectal temperature unless you've been trained to)</small>

Cotton, Gauze Pads _____

Cotton Swabs _____

Elastic (Ace) Bandages _____

Alcohol _____

Lotion Or Ointment For Stings _____

Baking Soda _____

Cough Medicine, Decongestant _____
<small>(follow parents' instructions for use)</small>

Earache Oil _____
<small>(for earache; follow parents' instructions for use)</small>

Nasal Aspirator _____
<small>(follow parents' instructions for use)</small>

Tweezers _____

Heating Pad _____

Other Supplies _____

_____

Allergy or Special Medical Information

(For notes on special medical or health-related conditions specific to the children and requiring certain cautions or restrictions.)

Child's Name _____

Condition _____

_____

Specific Instructions _____

_____

_____

Child's Name _____

Condition _____

_____

Specific Instructions _____

_____

_____

Child's Name _____

Condition _____

_____

Specific Instructions _____

_____

_____

Medical Treatment Form

Authorization to Consent to Treatment of a Minor

I (we), the undersigned parent(s)/guardian(s) of the minor(s) listed below, do hereby authorize

_____ or

(family doctor or pediatrician)

_____ or

(adult into whose care minor(s) is entrusted)

Emergency room physician in charge at:

_____

(name of children's or emergency hospital)

to act in my (our) place to consent to all necessary and appropriate X-ray examinations, anesthetic, medical or surgical diagnosis or treatment and hospital care which is deemed advisable by, and is to be rendered under the general or special supervision of any physician or surgeon licensed to

practice medicine under the laws of the state of _____ .

(this state)

It is understood that this authorization, which is valid for 12 months from the date below unless sooner terminated, is given in advance of any specific diagnosis, treatment or hospital care, but is given to provide authority and power on the part of my (our) aforesaid(s) to give specific consent to any and all such diagnosis, treatment or hospital care which the aforementioned physician in the exercise of their best medical judgment is deemed advisable, and is within sound medical practice in the community and is in the best interest of the child(ren).

I (we) assume all financial responsibility for the delivery of such care.

Child(ren)'s Name(s)	Birthdate	Blood Type	Allergies

Address and Phone _____

(Continued on p. 42)

41

Medical Treatment Form (cont.)

Doctor's Name _____ Phone _____

Name _____ Phone _____

Medical Insurance Company and Policy Number

Name _____ Policy No. _____

Signed _____
(mother and/or father)

_____
(legal guardian)

Date _____
(date of parent/guardian signature)

County of _____)
)ss.
State of _____)

Subscribed and sworn to
before me this _____ day of
_____ , _____ .

_____
(notary public)

Signed _____
(mother and/or father)

_____
(legal guardian)

Date _____
(date of parent/guardian signature when notarized)

Note: Many states require that "Power of Attorney" such as this be notarized. This form is accept-able in most states. Parents are advised to check with their physicians and hospitals for any changes necessary. It may also be advisable to give the family doctor or pediatrician a copy of the form.

Household Emergencies

In an emergency you can't handle alone, the best thing you can do is to get the right HELP. It's always better to be safe than sorry, and the parents will be glad to know that you've done what's necessary to cope with a situation beyond your control. Usually you'll start by calling the parents (or your parents or a neighbor if the parents aren't available).

If you get sick: Call the parents immediately so they can come home. If you're too ill to care for the children, or the parents can't be reached, call a neighbor or your own parents.

Fire: Don't try to put out a fire, even a little one. Get the children and get out immediately. Go to the nearest neighbor's to call the fire department. Don't try to use the elevator if you're in an apartment; use the stairway. THE FAMILY MEETING PLACE OUTSIDE THIS HOUSE IS _____
If any of the children go out separately, meet them there.

If you smell gas: Call the gas company (see p. ii for the number). Stay near an open window or door with the children until the serviceman comes.

Power outage: If power is out in just part of the house, it's probably a blown circuit breaker or fuse. If it's out all over the house, call the electric company (p. ii). Blackouts don't usually last for long, but if it's dark, reassure the children by getting out the flashlight. Light a few candles, perhaps, but be sure to put them high enough so small children can't reach them. Turn off the appliances and lights you know are on, but leave one light on so you'll know when power returns.

Storms, tornadoes: Stay inside and keep the children in. If the wind is very strong, go to the southwest corner of the basement or get under a sturdy table if that's not possible. Take a battery-operated radio with you for storm reports, and a flashlight, in case the power goes out. Stay away from windows.

Prowlers or a break-in: NEVER LET A STRANGER IN THE HOUSE. Don't hesitate to call the police (the number is on p. i) if you think prowlers are in the neighborhood or if teenagers are hanging about and bothering you. In case of an actual break-in, cooperate with the thief; don't try to be a hero. Your concern is the children, not household possessions: Call the police and the parents as soon as possible.

WHERE
TO FIND

Household
Emergency Equipment

Fire Extinguisher _____
(but if there's a fire, take the children and GET OUT!)

Water Shut-Off _____

Gas Shut-Off _____

Circuit Breaker or Fuse Box _____

Extra Fuses _____

Housekey, Money for Emergency Cab _____

Other Household Items

Flashlight, Batteries _____

Candles, Matches _____

Thermostat (and preferred setting) _____

Key or Tool to Unlock Bathroom Door from Outside _____

Vacuum Cleaner, Mop, Rags _____

Other Items You May Need

_____

_____

_____

_____

45

House Rules

(Parents may wish to pencil these in; rules change as children grow. Specific instructions for TODAY should be written out.)

Meals _____
(times, where eaten, special dishes and utensils, general routines)

_____

_____

_____

_____

Snacks _____
(where, when, what, what not)

_____

_____

_____

_____

Naptime _____
(times of day, routines)

_____

_____

_____

_____

Bedtime _____
(times, nightlight, door open/shut, special routines)

_____

_____

_____

_____

Chores, Duties _____
(Things children are expected to do themselves)

_____

_____

_____

_____

Pet Care _____
(in/out, leashed or not, feeding instructions)

_____

_____

_____

Playtime _____
(outdoors alone or not, activities allowed inside, "vehicle" rules)

_____

_____

_____

_____

Going To Others' Homes _____
(whose home, when, special instructions)

_____

_____

_____

_____

Havings Friends In _____
(who, if anyone; how many; when; special rules)

_____

_____

_____

TV Watching _____
(times, programs allowed, not allowed)

_____

_____

_____

_____

House Rules (cont.)

Other Rules _____

_____

_____

_____

_____

Always Off Limits! _____

_____

_____

_____

_____

Especially for Parents

As your sitter accepts the responsibility of caring for your children, you accept certain responsibilities toward your sitter.

- Tell a new sitter how many children you have, and let any sitter know if there will be additional visiting children to tend (upon hiring, not when he or she arrives!).

- Let the sitter know ahead of time if any of the children are sick.

- Make special arrangements with the sitter if you expect any housework to be done over and above cleaning up a "mess" created during the sitting period. Most parents pay extra for hours after midnight, too.

- Let your sitter know what's definitely "off limits" both for him or her and for the children so there will be no "surprises" for either of you.

- If you change your planned location while you are out, call home to leave the new phone number.

- Be prepared to pay the previously agreed-upon fee when you return, unless you've worked out another agreement ahead of time. Remember that teenagers sometimes find it hard to cash checks.

- Arrive home when you've said you will. If you're not going to be able to make it, call and let the sitter know when you will be there.

- Be in good condition to drive your sitter home.

- If you must cancel at the last minute, pay the sitter for the expected time, or at least for part of it.

Before You Leave

- Ask a first-time sitter to arrive early enough to get a thorough tour of your home and spend some time together with you and your child. (Be sure to include your child in the house tour, encouraging your little one's participation.) And let a baby first "get acquainted" from the safety of your arms before handing him or her to the sitter.

- Show your sitter how appliances and special furniture' such as a high chair with a tray lock, are used.

- If you're planning to call home and say good night to your child, let the sitter know when to expect your call.

- Encourage your sitter to play with your children rather than watch TV. (If you have TV-time-limit laws for your child, decide before your sitter's arrival whether or not you want them enforced.) Also, encourage sitters to bring their own games or ideas to entertain your child. Both sitter and child have more fun that way.

- Describe your child's bedtime routines and rituals (such as tooth-brushing, pajama parade, security blankets, pacifiers, or favorite bedtime stories), which make it easier for child and sitter alike.

- Warn your sitter of any normal delaying tactics your child may use at bedtime and how to deal with them. Suggest that active games—while good to release excess energy—should not be played just prior to bedtime, as they make it harder for a child to settle down to sleep.

- Suggest that older children be given advance warning of approaching bedtime so they can finish an activity or see the end of a TV show.

- Ask your sitter to check a sleeping child every hour or so, and to keep the TV and radio turned down so that a child who wakens can be heard.

Easing Separation Anxiety

Separation is hardest on children from' six months to two years of age. By six months, babies are old enough to know that you are unique and irreplaceable, but too young to understand that you are not disappearing forever when you go out the front door, despite your reassurances. Separation anxiety—expressed by crying and clinging—is a normal stage of development and a part of the growing-up process. Remind yourself of this at those hard-to-leave moments.

You can't always prevent your child's unhappiness about your leaving, but there are things you can do to minimize the stress. It helps to hire consistent caregivers—whether family members or neighborhood teens. This gives an extra feeling of security. Have your sitter come early—even after the first time—so your child has a chance to settle in with him or her, and so that the sitter is not perceived only as a stimulus for your departure. (If possible, have the sitter there at times when you will be home, too.)

Be forthright with your goodbyes even if the child seems unhappy. Don't sneak out the door, and never leave a sleeping child to wake up to a stranger. It may be painful to see your child cry, but honesty, even at this early age, is the best policy. On the other hand, prolonged goodbyes and extra reassurances will not lessen the distress, so leave promptly. Your child will most likely be fine once alone with the sitter. Most children settle down after the door closes behind their parents—or at least shortly thereafter.

Helping Your Child with Leave-Taking

- Advance notice of your departure helps a child prepare for even temporary separations.

- Talk about the sitter who is coming. Asking your child to make a special drawing for the sitter may increase interest in the sitter's arrival.

- Give your child concrete information about where you'll be and when you'll return, even if it's after he or she is asleep.

- Transitional objects such as security blankets and stuffed animals are often important aids to younger children. Welcome, rather than discourage, them.

- Establish your own rituals for departures. For instance, involve the child by asking for help in finding your coat or opening the door when you leave. Predictable routines make events easier for a child to manage.

- Leave a kiss implanted in your child's palm to "use when needed."

- Or leave a note or surprise for the sitter to share with your child during the time you are gone. Notes could contain references to your return.

Helping Your Sitter Handle
Separation Anxiety

- Provide an "ice breaker" activity, such as a game, book, or even a treasure hunt, to involve child and sitter and to shift attention away from your departure.

- Have your child show the sitter his or her bedroom and toys.

- If your child is slow to warm up, point out to the sitter a favorite toy, game or book. If the sitter begins to play alone with it, the child will usually join in.

- Save a favorite video or other treat for when the sitter comes. This will insure good feelings associated with that sitter.

- Suggest to the sitter that making something for the parents (such as a drawing) can help a child understand that the parents *will* return.

- Discuss plans for the next day to give a child something to look forward to and provide the assurance that tomorrow (and parents) will come. For instance, at bedtime, the sitter can mention breakfast with parents when the child wakes in the morning.

Remember that a child's difficulty with separation is usually not a reflection on the sitter's ability or even of the child's feelings about the sitter.

Babysitter Phone Directory

Name _____

Address _____ Phone _____

Notes _____

Name _____

Address _____ Phone _____

Notes _____

Name _____

Address _____ Phone _____

Notes _____

Name _____

Address _____ Phone _____

Notes _____

Name _____

Address _____ Phone _____

Notes _____

Babysitter Phone Directory

Name_____

Address_____ Phone_____

Notes_____

Name_____

Address_____ Phone_____

Notes_____

Name_____

Address_____ Phone_____

Notes_____

Name_____

Address_____ Phone_____

Notes_____

Name_____

Address_____ Phone_____

Notes_____

Babysitter Phone Directory

Name_____

Address_____ Phone_____

Notes_____

Name_____

Address_____ Phone_____

Notes_____

Name_____

Address_____ Phone_____

Notes_____

Name_____

Address_____ Phone_____

Notes_____

Name_____

Address_____ Phone_____

Notes_____

Babysitter Phone Directory

Name _____

Address _____ Phone _____

Notes _____

Name _____

Address _____ Phone _____

Notes _____

Name _____

Address _____ Phone _____

Notes _____

Name _____

Address _____ Phone _____

Notes _____

Name _____

Address _____ Phone _____

Notes _____

Other books by Vicki Lansky

- Feed Me I'm Yours
  - The Taming of the CANDY Monster
    - Practical Parenting Tips Yrs 1–5
      - Toilet Training
        - KoKo Bear's New Potty
          - Birthday Parties:Yrs 1-8
            - Welcoming Your
              Second Baby
              - A New Baby at
                KoKo Bear's House
                - KoKo Bear's
                  Big Earache
                - Getting Your
                  Child to Sleep...
                  and Back to Sleep
                  - Trouble-Free Travel
                    with Children

- Baby Proofing Basics • Dear Babysitter Handbook
- Divorce Book for Parents • 101 Ways to Tell Your
Child I Love You • 101 Ways to Make Your Child Feel
Special • 101 Ways to Say I Love You (for adults)
• 101 Ways to be a Special Dad • 101 Ways to be a
Special Mom • Kids Cooking • Microwave Cooking
for Kids • Games Babies Play From Birth To Twelve
Months • ANOTHER USE FOR... 101 Common Household
Items • Don't Throw That Out! A Pennywise Parent's
Guide to Creative Uses for Over 200 Household Items

For a free catalog of all Vicki's books or to order books,
Call 1-800-255-3379 or write
Practical Parenting Books-By-Mail
Dept. DBS, 15245 Minnetonka Blvd.
Minnetonka, MN 55345